It's Here Somewhere
and Other Poems

James W. Swinehart

It's Here Somewhere and Other Poems
Copyright © 2021 James W. Swinehart
All rights reserved.

No part of this publication may be reproduced, stored in a retrieval system, or transmitted, in any form or by any means, electronic, mechanical, photocopying, recording, or otherwise, without the prior written permission of the publisher.
Published in the United States of America.

Cover painting by James W. Swinehart
Cover and Interior design by Siori Kitajima,
SF AppWorks LLC SFAppWorks.com

Cataloging-in-Publication data for this book
is available from the Library of Congress.
ISBN-13:
Paperback: 978-1-950154-49-4
eBook: 978-1-950154-55-5

Published by The Sager Group LLC
TheSagerGroup.net

It's Here Somewhere
and Other Poems

James W. Swinehart

Table Of Contents

Preface xi

History 1
   A Dilemma On The Ark... 3
   The King Speaks 5

Current Events 7
   Thank You For Waiting, Your Grace 9
   A Small Change..11
   Lines 13
   You Slay Me 15
   How About Them Apples 19

Aging And Beyond 21
   A Reunion Verse 23
   Nice To See You Again, I Think 25
   A College Reunion Verse 27
   Longevity...29
   Trees And Us 31
   Just Wait 33
   Departure Lounge Comfort.......................................35
   Excesses For A Eulogy 37
   Halfway Home..39
   The Bright Side Of The Other Side 41
   Not So Famous Last Words 43
   Conversion 45

Coping With Modern Life 47
    Parking Meter Minutes 49
    The Optimist 51
    Down Time 53
    Winning 55
    Treadmill 57
    Sally 59
    Help 61

Authors, Writing, Books 63
    Fifty Shades of Green 65
    First Impressions Last 67
    Dan The Writer, Or Not 69
    Victor Hugo 71
    Where Books Go 73
    Anonymous 75
    Fair Game 77
    Miracle 79
    Lost Words 81
    Counting The Days 83

Personal Problems 85
    Prices May Vary 87
    It's Here Somewhere 89
    Oops 91
    Alas, Not Mine 93
    No Thanks, I'm Just Browsing 95
    Not Yet, Not Yet 97
    Insects Aside 99
    Geraniums 101

The Bargain 103
Well, Maybe Just One 105
Frustration 107

Idle Thoughts 109
Cowboy Hat 111
Not Every October Sky Is Blue 113
Toil And Trouble 115
Glass 117
Some Things I'm Grateful For 119
Necessities...121
Flattery 123
Lucky You 125
Aquarium 127
Unique 129
Thanksgiving 131
You And Me, Maybe 133
Friends 135
Feeling Better 137
Letting Go...139
Sometimes A Fence Makes Better Sense 141

Parenting..143
Cheese Power 145
Another Gift... 147

Fun With Words 149
Two Secure Workplaces...151
Causing A Flutter 153
Snow Job 155

- Venus 157
- What Is An Elevator Going Down? 159
- Pete 161
- Faith 163
- Variety 165
- Waving Hello 167
- The Skill Set 169
- The Painter's Eye 171
- Snookered 173
- Clever Hands 175
- Here's To You 177
- Protection 179
- Into The Sunset 181
- I'll Have Seconds, Please 183
- Grace 185
- Tom 187

Valentines 189

- Other Men's Dreams 191
- To The Woman Of The Year 193
- To My Misnamed Love 195
- Sure Comedy's Hard, But So Is Accounting 197
- The Pairs Competition 199
- One Risky Valentine 201
- Valentine's Day, Back So Soon 205
- Who Knew? 207
- Yes, I Take It Personally 209
- Heartthrob 211
- Wondering, Wondering 213

Let's Move Valentine's Day 215
Let's Look Back 217
Prothalamion For Us 219

Tom Swifties 221

About the Author 235

About the Publisher 237

Preface

We like to think we create the combinations of words that make up our sentences and more. This is true, but all of us have been exposed to multitudes of words that may influence our choice of an adjective, the decision to place a conjunction here rather than there, or the idea that rhyming a particular pair of words will work better than a dozen alternatives.

We may be unaware of these connections, but it seems fair to acknowledge the debt we owe to the authors and poets whose words have lifted our spirits and sometimes changed lives across years and even centuries. I also want to thank my parents, for a house with plenty of books and encouragement to learn everything, and the teachers of English and literature and drama who fostered appreciation and awe at what precision and imagination could achieve.

For this particular book, I warmly thank Brian and Tricia Swinehart for making it possible. I am also grateful to the New Rochelle residents and others who came to public readings over the last few years, at the public library and coffee shops and elsewhere, and laughed (at least sometimes) at the right places. For the section on valentines, all of which and a good many more were written for my wife, Sandra, during our half-century together, my gratitude will be apparent on every page.

I hope readers will feel an urge to read some of these verses to a friend or family member. While my first title, "Some Smiles to Share," had already been used, the sentiment remains.

—James W. Swinehart

History

A Dilemma On The Ark

A single earthworm, fully grown,
Can reproduce although alone,
Because the organs of both sexes
Reside within its solar plexus.
Thus it may not need to mate
In order to proliferate.

So Noah asked, "Should I take Two?
For the worms just one should do,
But no one mentioned an exception
For hermaphrodite conception.
To follow orders yet be fair,
Should I choose one or take a pair?"

He thought the former, then the latter,
But in the end it didn't matter.
Whatever number went aboard
Was bound to satisfy the Lord:
Whether single or a deuce,
Worms were sure to reproduce.

Since either choice left Noah vexed
By overpopulated decks,
He felt that future holy texts
Should warn that worms are oversexed.

The King Speaks

"Pray take this purse, and hie thee thither,
Procuring at once a gooseberry pie.
Return anon, hastening hither,
Tarrying not until thou art nigh.

"Taste not the pie along the way,
Lest it arrive here less than whole.
Mark me well, or rue the day
And forfeit both thy life and soul.

"A pie that's rendered incomplete
Hath less appeal than one untasted.
Sirrah, thy transit must be fleet.
Thou cans't not let an hour be wasted."

The king hungered for pie yet he feared indigestion.
He mused, "To eat, or not to eat – that is the question."

(The King Speaks: Postscript)

The pie came on time and was eaten with dinner.
The king, with surprise, said "It made me no thinner!"
Dieticians who proposed that pie should be eaten
Were promptly dragged off to the dungeon and beaten.

Alas, although kings have the power to ransom,
Pies are unlikely to make them more handsome.
Despite having freedom to eat what they please,
Their bodies profit more from carrots and peas.

Still, royals get pie while the masses get bread.
We distinguish the two by the way they are fed.
Though kings seldom diet, we ought to forgive them –
The odds say we peasants may well outlive them.

Current Events

Thank You For Waiting, Your Grace

Hamlet, a prince, once famously said
"The time is out of joint."
Happenings in England now
Would seem to prove his point.

The press says Queen Elizabeth Two,
Now ninety-four, may rule forever,
So the current prince may get the crown
Around the first of never.

The Duke of Cornwall, Prince of Wales,
Heir apparent since the age of three,
Has grown up anticipating
A reign that he may never see.

Charles, now seventy-two,
Some years past the age of retirement.
He's learned that for the position of King
Experience is not a requirement.

The prince is said to be patient,
But is finding it hard to believe
That he's spent a lifetime awaiting
A job he may never receive.

Though the Queen does not doubt his judgment –
Not at iota, a whit, or scintilla –
She may have asked friends if a rational man
Would trade a Diana for a Camilla.

Whatever the reason, she may keep the crown;
At least that would seem her intention.
She continues to enjoy being the Queen,
And says Charles can live well on his pension.

A Small Change

I'm not sure why, but it seems a crime
That a nickel is twice as big as a dime.
If you were going just by touch
You'd value it at twice as much.
Perhaps someone could drop a hint
To officials at the U.S. mint:
The use of graduated dies
Would let value correspond to size.

Alas, these people, as you've heard,
Do something you may find absurd:
They pay two cents to make each penny.
Does that make sense? Hardly any.

So I won't wait for larger dimes
Or nickels to get somewhat smaller.
Though sanity may come in time,
By then these coins may cost a dollar.

Lines

Words across a parchment page
two centuries ago
   ...that all men are created equal...

Words of youth and strength
on a cold January day
   ...We will bear any burden...

Words of vision and hope
to overcome exclusion and fear
   ...I have a dream...

And more than words
Lines of markers, starkly white
on endless fields of green
in Arlington and far beyond.
Lines of names on a granite wall
to touch and remember.

On election day, by twos and tens,
then thousands, and millions,
the lines in places large and small
spoke their own truth
about our debt, and our promise:
   One nation, indivisible.
   From many, one.

You Slay Me

The news of recent executions
That were botched or went awry
Have led proponents to avow
That they would diligently try
To find a way that worked each time
So punishment could fit the crime,
A way that was confirmed as lawful
But not leave viewers feeling awful.
Chemical cocktails, it's undeniable,
Have proved to be unreliable.

Although to some it seems insane
to make these killings more humane,
Proponents say they're civilized
When victims are anesthetized,
And all agree we should make certain
That when they drop that final curtain
It must be demonstrably clear
That the person is no longer here.
Since this problem can't be ignored,
Alternatives must be explored.

One way would be to give the nod
To employment of a firing squad.
That works but one flaw gives us pause:
It violates noise abatement laws.

Or surround the felon with some folks
Who are masterful at telling jokes;
The comics might find they were thrilled
To learn that they had really killed.

Or the sentence could be carried out
In another way that leaves no doubt:
Transport him to a distant land
Inhabited by a primitive band
Of cannibals who would ask the sinner
If he would please drop by for dinner.

If a jury says, "Off with his head!"
That's one way to make sure he's dead.
To manage that, as some have seen,
We could resurrect the guillotine.
No victim ever has complained
That it caused him undue pain,
Or that its use was clearly wrong
Since killing him took much too long.

Perhaps it would allay our frowning
If we gave some thought to drowning,
And for this grim, unpleasant job,
We hired some hit men from the mob.
They might be glad to find a use
For their supply of concrete shoes.

If sky diving's on his bucket list,
One step will make sure he's missed:
To guarantee it's effective,
Use a parachute that's defective.

Some have plumped for suicide,
But that solution can't be tried.
There are moral objections, and
Prison suicides are banned.
We can't give a rope and leave him to it —
His death won't count unless we do it.

But after his final meal of choice,
Cholesterol might still his voice.
If his veins were clogged or porous
A heart attack might kill him for us.
If we let nature take its course
We'd have no need to feel remorse.

In centuries past a clear plurality
Believed it would promote morality
To hold executions in public squares
With a festive air, like county fairs.
Though the public may someday be willing
To disavow official killing,
Until that time let's seek to gain
Better ways to be entertained.

How About Them Apples

*(A recent November: A group of raccoons
in West Virginia got drunk on crab apples
and caused a rabies scare. Police said
they were "staggering and disoriented,"
so were held in custody to sober up
before being returned to the wild.)*

The cops saw raccoons
Wobbling and weaving,
Smiling broadly and showing
No interest in leaving.

One cop said their masks
Signaled evil intention,
And preventing a theft
Might require detention.

So the black-and-white rodents
Rode in black-and-white cars,
Facing possible arrest
And some time behind bars.

When their breathing was tested
And alcohol levels obtained,
Each one topped the limit
So they all were detained.

In the morning they were freed
To return to the woods,
Hoping never again
To be mistaken for hoods.

Aging And Beyond

A Reunion Verse

I don't have what I used to —
for example, my hair.
And I may need a boost to
get out of my chair.

My memory plays tricks.
I'm no longer zestful.
What I do for kicks
most people find restful.

My arms and legs no longer grow,
except to grow more nervous
when they recall how long ago
they were placed in service.

But the years have been kind
to the girls here, now prettier,
And the boys are inclined
to seem stronger, and wittier.

We've known joys and sorrows,
had children, and weaned them.
We believe in tomorrows
though no one has seen them.
So old and dear friends,
be glad we're still here.
If your knees will still bend,
you can stand up and cheer.

(I meant to write more
this happy September.
I probably did but
I just can't remember.)

Nice To See You Again, I Think

We come to reunions
Hopeful but unsure –
Will friends think I look old
Or just more mature?

But we shouldn't worry
Since it's easy to tell
That these judging friends
Can't see very well.

It's also reassuring
And undeniably true
That the changes in us
Have affected them, too.

And the much larger truth,
Physical changes aside,
Is that we remain
The same people inside.

We're still who we were
Perhaps even more so.
Our eyes show our essence,
Much more than our torso.

Inside we're the same
As we were long ago,
But forgive me for asking –
Are you someone I know?

A College Reunion Verse

We return again to our old school,
Lasting home of our mental fuel,
The start of our knowledge intellectual,
Philosophical, psychosexual.
It's true we've scattered far and wide,
But the college knows we cannot hide.
Where'ere we go they're sure to find us
And send a letter to remind us
That whether days be dark or sunny,
The need is constant. Please send money.

Longevity

I envy my Town Resident card
Because it lacks something I hate.
It has my name and my picture,
But unlike me, no expiration date.

This prompted a look at my passport,
And I found that it lapsed years ago.
If that means my trip should have ended,
That's something I'd rather not know.

So I rummaged around in my wallet
And found something to lessen my fears.
If my driver's license means what it says,
I'm entitled to seven more years.

Trees And Us

(News item: Chestnuts and many other trees live
100 years or longer.)

I think that I shall never see
our life-span match that of a tree.
Though they lose leaves and we lose hair,
and on the surface that seems fair,
they get more with each new spring
while we get less of everything.

I don't say a graceful pine
should have a life as short as mine,
but if a tree can live so long
what could possibly be wrong
with extra years for you and me
so we could match the average tree?

Just Wait

As my uncle went into his nineties,
He was asked how it felt to grow old.
He said "On balance I'm happy to be here,
But the benefits have been oversold.

"Friends claimed that aging needn't cause harm.
They said there's no reason to fear it.
But I bought a watch that has an alarm,
And now I can't hear it.

"I asked those friends what things they liked best
But the older ones had to demur.
Those in the best position to know
Could no longer recall what they were.

"Some say that people grow wiser with age
But don't believe all that you hear.
The number of things that we know for sure
Grows smaller with each passing year.

"For example, we used to take for granted
That Pluto would always be a planet.
And we're quite amazed, so please forgive us,
At light bulbs guaranteed to outlive us.

"This isn't to say that we can't accept change;
We have done that for decades gone by.
But we fondly recall how things used to be
And ask if transformation is needed, and why."

Departure Lounge Comfort

Ashes to ashes
And dust to dust.
The thought depresses
But God is just:

No more rents
And no more dues.
No fender dents.
No painful shoes.

No traffic jams
Or ringing phones.
No flooding dams
Or unpaid loans.

No more colds
Or hacking cough.
No more hard rolls
That should be soft.

No more aches
And no more pains.
No earthquakes
Or pouring rains.

No itchy rashes
Or nails that bend.
No airplane crashes
Or clothes to mend.

Of course we'd rather stay. This list
Is not to make us queasier,
But pondering some things not missed
May make departing easier.

Excesses For A Eulogy

He danced too many dances
and sang too many songs.
He took too many chances,
righted too many wrongs.

He spent too much time with friends,
dried too many children's tears.
Celebrated too many wins,
overcame too many fears.

He was kissed too many times
And hugged too often, too.
He enjoyed too many rhymes,
ate too much tasty stew.

He petted too many cats and dogs,
never settled for second best,
Sat by too many fireplace logs,
and sniffed perfume to excess.

He ate too much ice cream,
accompanied by cakes.
Fulfilled too many dreams,
swam in too many lakes.

He smiled too many smiles,
and laughed too many laughs,
Hiked too many miles,
ignored too many gaffes.

If you think I've misconstrued
opportunities that were missed,
Consider all these things not rued
and make up your own list.

Halfway Home

Of course it leaves me feeling good
To do what people say I should.
It's satisfying to be caught
Doing things I know I ought,
Winning smiles and earning plaudits,
Never fearing moral audits.

But I confess I also treasure
Other things that bring me pleasure,
Some of which, while not forbidden,
Are unannounced and may be hidden.
In fact they may not quite comport
With morals of the public sort.

So pulled both ways, my life's a riddle
Solved by choosing in the middle:
Neither sinning nor quite saintly,
Observing strictures seen but faintly,
Seeking good but failing often,
Watching my firm virtues soften.

When Judgment Day is facing me
And God reviews my history,
My best hope may sound unhinged:
To get to heaven barely singed.
Unless, like me, He splits the difference
And chooses limbo as my sentence.

The Bright Side Of The Other Side

Here lies the royal William
Who was once a noble king,
Resting here without his scepter
Or his signet ring.

His power is now held by his heirs,
His land and castles, too.
The world that once lay at his feet
Has disappeared from view.

But does he mourn the wealth he's lost
Or songs he used to sing?
Some would say the good news is
He doesn't miss a thing.

Not So Famous Last Words

Do you believe me now?
That was exciting – really got my heart pumping.
C'mon, shoveling the snow should be easy.
I forget – is it starve a fever, feed a cold?
I can't find the safety switch.
Is this thing plugged in?
We're safe — lightning has already struck here.
No longer worried about my weight.
Thanks for visiting. Please come again.
Oops.

Conversion

I woke up feeling very warm, and
blurted out, "Where the hell am I?"
A man standing nearby said, "Good
guess." I asked him if those bagpipes
were playing all the time. He said, "All
day, every day. And on weekends we have
Schoenberg concerts." I said I didn't believe
in Hell before, but I was now a believer, so I
didn't belong there. He said "I'll tell the boss.
He loves irony. Goodbye."

Coping With Modern Life

Parking Meter Minutes

Sometimes I find a parking space
That makes my spirits lift.
A meter with some minutes left
Is an unexpected gift.

Drivers that have overpaid
Are gone and can't be thanked.
They have to leave the extra time
Since minutes can't be banked.

I may use a credit card
To add some extra time,
Though now I pay real money for
What used to cost a dime.

If I should come back early
And leave some time behind,
The next guy parks free for a while
But I certainly won't mind.

After all, tomorrow
My turn may come again
With minutes in my favor
That I'll tally as a win.

It's kind of like when neighbors' leaves
Land in my yard, in piles or sparely –
The next day they blow back to theirs,
So in time we all get treated fairly.

The Optimist

George chose to look on the bright side
When a flood caused his house to float.
He said "I no longer have an address,
But I've always wanted a boat."

Down Time

Beth was on hold for so long
She no longer knew what to do.
She decided to pray for assistance,
But found that line was busy, too.

Winning

His friends said his schemes to save money
Were so extreme that he must be demented,
But he had the last laugh when he died –
The suit he was buried in was rented.

Treadmill

It's true a treadmill sits untouched
In my household's darkest place,
Untapped for fitness purposes
Or training for a race.

It's kind of like insurance,
Which is costly on its face —
I hope I'll never need it
But I have it just in case.

Sally

Sally was frustrated by her TV,
Never knowing which programs to choose.
Cooking shows upset her digestion;
She grew anxious watching the news.
Thinking of all the shows that were on,
She found a way to become less annoyed.
Rather than selecting those she would watch,
She made a list of the ones to avoid.

Help

What we're often advised to do
In emergencies makes me smile —
They tell us to dial nine-one-one
But our phones don't have a dial.

Authors, Writing, Books

Fifty Shades of Green

News item: *The novel "Fifty Shades of Grey" earned more than $100 million in its first year, and sequels trebled that amount.*

They say a woman named E. L. James
Wrote a book about erotic games.
It sold so well, or so I've heard,
She wrote another, and then a third
About a rich guy and naïve honey
That brought her endless piles of money.

Critics called the writing awful,
Bad enough to be unlawful –
Paragraphs on tailored jeans,
Private jets and limousines,
Descriptions of a manly torso,
And a woman's, only more so.

Reviews made note of leather whips,
Negligees and moistened lips,
Tales of handcuffs on her wrists
That somehow got her touched and kissed,
All read by women drawn to cads
Who take control in high-rise pads.

When sex is won through stick or carrot,
Erotica can help us share it,
And characters without a stitch
Often make their authors rich —
But some books sold for heaps of cash
May still be classified as trash.

Though James lucked out and we did not,
We shouldn't envy what she's got.
She earns my praise for great success
Though this is tempered, I confess.
And I'll admit to one more sin:
I'd smile if someone did her in.

First Impressions Last

Artists who work for publishers
Seek to persuade every book lover
To upend the adage, and entice us
To judge any book by its cover.

Though readers may doubt their success,
Proud authors confront a sad fact:
Collectors who never open their books
Pay more if the jackets are intact.

Dan The Writer, Or Not

Dan wanted to become a writer,
But he needed an agent to start.
A friend said it wouldn't be easy,
But try to find one with a heart.

Since new writers' earnings are slim,
His dealings with agents were tough.
Though he offered them half of his income,
They said <u>all</u> of it won't be enough.

That's how he learned that ambition
And talent and luck and persistence
Were vital but no guarantee
That a book would come into existence.

So the novels that he might have written
On space travel or original sin
Will not be displayed in a bookstore
Or end up in their remainder bin.

And the ones that might have earned prizes,
Bringing him fortune and fame,
Will never see print between covers,
Their fate exactly the same.

Victor Hugo

When Victor Hugo wrote "Les Miserables,"
He won millions of readers' loyalties,
But because he died decades too soon,
Others are collecting his royalties.

Where Books Go

Some people sort their books by author,
Others by color or title.
For some, covers govern the placement,
While others see the contents as vital.

I tried to sort my books by topic,
But learned I was fooling myself
When fantasy titles and politics
Were neighbors on the same shelf.

Anonymous

Publishers tend to love books
Anonymously written
And issued in the hope that
Some readers will be smitten.

They're not bothered by the fact
That critics often trash them,
Since royalty checks are nameless
And authors cannot cash them.

Fair Game

Some authors at the book fair
Were giving me peevish looks,
Annoyed by my new best-seller,
"How to Avoid Self-Help Books."

Miracle

Twenty-four centuries ago,
a man named Aristophanes
had an idea for a comedy. Thoughts
moved to his hands, and he wrote
some words on papyrus or vellum,
then many more words, and finally
decided the work was done.

Hundreds of years passed, with
many chances for the words
to be lost, to disappear between
generations as wars and floods
and plagues destroyed people
and countries and ideas. But
somehow, though by then
the words were only bits of ink
on paper, they survived.

This year, half a world away
from Greece and now in
another language, those words
made people in a theater laugh
because they understood and felt
what one man wanted them
to understand and feel
when he wrote so long ago.

If this impossible thing happened once,
we'd say it's astonishing. When it
happens a thousand times, we can say
if that's not a miracle,
there are no miracles.

Lost Words

When my dictionary disappeared,
I said this is quite absurd –
But at last I knew what it could mean
To be at a loss for words.

I still had good intentions,
But things went from bad to worse.
Lacking a vocabulary,
I could only write blank verse.

Counting The Days

James Russell Lowell, perhaps speaking too soon,
Asked what is so rare as a day in June.
Though other months' days may seldom be fairer,
As a shorter month February days must be rarer.

Creativity is encouraged, but within reason.
Lowell must have known that days vary by season.
Poetic license gives flexibility, but surely
It seems that his was conferred prematurely.

Personal Problems

Prices May Vary

They said money can't buy happiness,
So I didn't save money — I spent it.
I confirmed that happiness wasn't for sale,
But found out too late I could rent it.

It's Here Somewhere

I bought a book on memory
And eagerly embraced it.
I meant to read it right away
But seem to have misplaced it.

It claims to offer good advice
And I intend to mind it.
I plan to do that right away,
Just as soon as I can find it.

You're telling me to look for it,
That I obviously need it.
I realize that. Get off my case.
When it turns up I will read it.

Oops

I recently got some advice to tone up
That unsurprisingly came from my spouse.
So I ordered some weights and was ready to start,
But couldn't carry them into the house.

Alas, Not Mine

Since others often have something that I may covet,
I'm dismayed when they tell me how much they love it.
For example, my neighbor's house has many more rooms,
and his garden is always a showplace of blooms.
His trees are taller, his bushes bushier,
And I suspect that his tush is tushier.
His car is much newer, and of course sleeker,
His knowledge of Plato is known to be Greeker.
The meals he cooks deserve three stars or higher.
When the market is rising he's always a buyer.
The children of genius include those he's sired.
Nobelists are among the people he's hired.
His disposition is moderately sunnier,
And all would agree that his jokes are funnier.
But in one respect he is clearly no whiz —
My envy will always be greener than his.

No Thanks, I'm Just Browsing

Eyebrows, it's said, shield our eyes from the rain,
But also tell friends that we're glad or in pain.
They let others know when we're angry or quizzical,
So it's clear that their purpose is not simply physical.
They seldom deserve any notice or mention,
But some can find ways to attract our attention.

On most days my face won't concern me unduly,
But lately my eyebrows have grown quite unruly.
Some hairs have turned up in places they shouldn't,
While others fall out when they normally wouldn't.
Some are now straight that used to be curly,
And some without patience have left prematurely.

Some have turned curly that used to be straight,
Others, more cautious, have chosen to wait
While I figure out what procedure will work
To make these small thickets appear less berserk.

My preference would be to simply ignore them,
Or have them removed and somehow restore them
By transplanting hairs from my ears and my nose
Where their unwanted growth just adds to my woes.
Weaving them into two tiny toupees
Would make my face neater in multiple ways.

Not Yet, Not Yet

My intention is firm,
But I can see why you scoff.
I mean to procrastinate
But keep putting it off.

I tried to delay vacation,
But ended up just wishing.
A friend said "Carpe Diem" meant
Today we should go fishing.

Now I plan to start anew
This morning or this afternoon,
But if some pressing tasks arise,
I may say "Not yet, but soon."

I've tried to postpone everything
But am learning to my sorrow,
Some things can't be put off today.
Perhaps I'll try tomorrow.

Insects Aside

Everyone knows insects are useful,
To birds and plants everywhere.
Though I don't question their value,
My home has more than its share.

Last summer flies came in my house
Through an opening by a door.
There were just a few at first,
Then there were plenty more.

Mosquitoes also haunt my yard,
Buzzing by my ears,
Threatening diseases,
Arousing primal fears.

Moths live in my closet,
Munching on my clothes.
They leave remnants on the floor
Aligned in linty rows.

Ants march on my kitchen floor,
Wasps live in my eaves.
Chiggers crawl inside my shirt
When I'm out raking leaves.
Many bugs have come to stay —
Like aphids, ticks, and gnats.
They all seem to think that I've
Put out some welcome mats.

I'm hoping when cold weather comes
They'll head for warmer climes.
To echo Dickens, that would be
For me the best of times.

If icy air makes mites and bees
Depart for Tennessee,
I guarantee that December
Can't come soon enough for me.

Geraniums

My geraniums persisted in staying green
But I learned they were just playing possum.
When offered plenty of water and sun
They perked up and started to blossom.

I thought a new kind might have more appeal
And so I decided to cross 'em.
The experiment was clearly worth trying
But it failed, and I had to toss 'em.

The Bargain

I was browsing at a store
When a poster caught my eye:
A case of Alpo priced so low
I couldn't pass it by.

I hurried home to tell my wife
I'd saved a bunch of money.
And she replied, "Hey, good for you,
But listen to me, honey:

I hope this won't upset you
But your brain is in a fog.
You don't have a pedigree
And we don't own a dog."

Well, Maybe Just One

Your beauty, plus a little gin,
Makes my will go weak and hollow.
I won't lead you into sin,
But I'm almost sure to follow.

Frustration

Somehow I never got the hang
Of throwing away a boomerang.
It seems I've also lost the knack
Of telling an echo, "Don't call back."

With sales calls it's much the same,
Though callers never know my name.
I haven't stopped more than a few
By saying "Next time I'll call you."

Idle Thoughts

Cowboy Hat

The voice has faded in ole' Garth Brooks
But the crowds still like his cowboy looks

If I had a hat with a five-inch brim
The odds are I could sing like him

I know that I could sing like that
If I only had a cowboy hat

I don't care if the hat's black or white
It would make me a hero on Saturday night

If I had a hat with a crease in the middle
And a countrified pal with boots and a fiddle

I'd have a style like Waylon Jennings
And girls would scream for extra innings

Like Willie Nelson, I could hold the stage
Wearing a hat that's half my age

With a cowboy hat like Conway Twitty's
I'd be famous in towns and cities

If I had a hat with a brim that curls
I'd be up to my ears in girls

A wide black hat like ole' George Strait's
Would get me multitudes of dates

It's true my voice won't take me far
But with a cowboy hat I'd be a star

Not Every October Sky Is Blue

Gloom, and absent shadows,
crowd the space under trees
and beside buildings. We breathe
the thick and wet stuff
of air; thick and wet, it hides
everywhere. Sodden are the
gray leaves, dull leaves, brown leaves,
soaked with the tasteless damp
of an autumn rain. No spark of sunlight
sees these leaves as they stagger and fall –
worn, tattered pages of a rich and open book,
falling, falling, falling
down
With raindrops as their tears.

Toil And Trouble

One never knows where dangers lurk,
But given global warming trends
Glaciologists may be out of work
Well before our world ends.

Glass

If there were no glass
We might wonder what we look like
And thus maybe even who we are
Because there would be no mirrors.
Every room would be dark in the day
Because there would be no windows
And dark at night because
No lights would replace the sun.
We would wonder about the bright spots
In the sky at night because without telescopes
Stars and planets would keep their mystery.
We would be unaware of the tiny things in our bodies
That make us sick or keep us well
Because there would be no microscopes.
We would have to drive very slowly
Because cars would have no windshields,
And never at night because
There would be no headlights or street lights.
Many people would give up books
And newspapers and letters from friends
Because there would be no reading glasses.
Without screens for computers and TV sets
We would have more time, but might lose track

Of that because clocks and watches and
Smartphones would have no faces.
Houses of worship would lose the glory of
stained glass, and the brilliance of crystal vases
and chandeliers would be no more.

From heat and opaque sand
Somehow came transparency
In an amorphous solid that is
Such a puzzle for science
That even if you could see it,
It would be hard to believe.

Some Things I'm Grateful For

EARS – they keep our glasses from falling off.
STAIRS AND ELEVATORS – without them, every building would be only one story high, there would be no basements or attics to put stuff in, our cities would be very spread out, and skylines would all look alike.
ROUND WHEELS – if they were square or even octagonal, it would take a long time to get anywhere and the ride would be really rough.
THE FACT THAT GRASS IS GREEN – it is nice to look at a park or field or pasture, but wouldn't be so restful on the eyes if it were orange or pink.
THE FACT THAT WATER RUNS DOWNHILL – if it didn't, sinks and toilets would be a big problem, flooded streets would never drain, raindrops would just hang around in the air, and we would have to use a straw to drink anything.
PERSIMMONS – they are sour, and avoiding them is a source of pleasure.

Necessities

It has often been said that the necessities of life
are food, clothing, and shelter.
Yet over millennia, in every time and place, people
have drawn pictures.
And they have made music.
And they have danced.
Maybe it's time to admit that three necessities are
not enough.

Flattery

Some people say the world is flat
And if you stand on the edge
Anywhere at all
And your hat blows off
You will never get it back.
But if you tossed a coin over, like into a fountain,
Would that mean you would return someday?
Maybe not. I'm glad the world is round
So I won't lose my hat, or a coin, or myself.

Lucky You

If you don't drive a convertible
And you don't own a boat
Or have a beach house
Or a backyard pool
Or belong to a country club
Or vacation in Aruba
You are less likely to get skin cancer

Aquarium

If you asked a goldfish
What the world is like
It might be likely to say
The world has four sides
That are smooth and clear
But anyplace outside is blurry
What's above is sometimes wavy
Everyone is orange and has fins
Once or twice a day
Food falls from the sky
You don't have to work for it
But every day you wonder
If it will come again tomorrow
Of course what a goldfish is
Really most likely to say is
Blup.

Unique

Seven billion people on the earth
Each like every other in uncountable ways
But each different in some way
From every other.
How odd it seems
That the one thing we all have in common
Is that we are all different.

Thanksgiving

People feel good about donating food
And sharing their nice way of living
But some seem to feel that the poor
Get hungry only at Thanksgiving

You And Me, Maybe

It's not the house you live in,
It's not the clothes you wear.
It's not the kind of car you drive,
Or how you style your hair.
It's what's inside that I like most,
The you that makes me care.
Now how about some praise for me –
Don't you think that would be fair?
I think our pedestals should match,
If we're going to become a pair.

Friends

As we journey through life, we hope to make friends –
Some closer than others, not all the same.
Ever wonder how many good friends you have?
Count the ones who remember your middle name.

Feeling Better

Some people are always complaining –
Feeling sorry they aren't yet rich.
But scratching wouldn't feel nearly so good
If they weren't first having an itch.

Letting Go

Relations may sour, friendships may fade;
If people fall out, I'm not one to judge.
But care must be taken, attention be paid
To the seven-year limit on holding a grudge.

Sometimes A Fence Makes Better Sense

The highway crews installed "Deer Crossing" signs
In hopes of reducing car-deer collisions,
But the signs often had little effect
On the deer or the drivers' decisions.
The drivers still felt entitled to speed,
Confident that deer were unable to read.

Parenting

G. K. Chesterton once wrote, "*Poets have been mysteriously silent on the subject of cheese.*" Well, no longer.

Cheese Power

Parents who want their kids to eat peas
Too seldom employ the power of cheese,
They also may miss a hug or a kiss
By failing to offer a bribe of swiss.

When the kids won't eat but one must feed 'em,
Break out some gouda, or maybe edam.
If they spend too much time on their phone,
Threaten to reduce their provolone.

If they skip their lessons on piano,
Warn them that means less romano.
To encourage homework you should see
That progress comes from offering brie.

If they won't study Sartre or Savonarola,
Incentivize them with gorgonzola.
Sometimes results may be even better
If rewards are toast with melted cheddar.

If they say that's ordinary or unfair,
Offer them chunks of camembert.
A bored son can be a happy fella

When given sticks of mozzarella,
And children whether large or small
Are known to thrive on emmental.

Though every battle won't be won,
Wise use of cheese may get it done.
It may not work as well as pie
But you won't know until you try.
Nothing will work every time,
As there are no guarantees.
But you can often fetch a smile
With just two magic words: "Say cheese."

Another Gift

Before we had children,
I discussed with my wife
how we could help them
be successful in life.

So they'd be known by their own
and not someone else's name,
we chose not to burden them
with parental fame.

I'm glad to report that
I managed to achieve it —
Each time success threatened,
I would walk off and leave it.

As a blessing for my kids,
fame and fortune eluded me.
Annual editions of *Who's Who*
consistently excluded me.

My greatest success came
from pushing achievement aside,
so my children could develop
their own reasons for pride.

I thought they'd be grateful
but instead they exhort us:
if we'd put more in the bank,
they wouldn't have to support us.

Fun With Words

Two Secure Workplaces

The occupations of jailer and jeweler
Sound alike but are differently spelled.
You can distinguish them because the jailer
Is the one who at work watches cells.

Causing A Flutter

When scientists cloned a sheep,
They created Dolly without a mother.
Perhaps they could do this with shore birds
Since one good tern deserves another.

Snow Job

The neighborhood kids made a large ball of snow,
Then another, and put it above number one.
A small one was placed on top of the second.
They added a face, and then they were done.
It looked odd with the largest ball in the middle --
Was this a mistake, or meant as a riddle?
The kids said "This isn't an error, oh no, man,
Our aim was to make abdominal snowman."

Venus

The beautiful torso of Venus de Milo
Was carved about one hundred B.C.
It was found two millennia later
On an isle in the Agean Sea.
Visitors who see it displayed in the Louvre
Have admired it for ten generations,
Undismayed by the losses that made it
The most famous statue of limitations.

What Is An Elevator Going Down?

The name given to an elevator
Is wrong enough to prompt a frown:
It signifies carrying passengers up
But it ignores taking them down.

When their name is partially right
But their function is omitted by half,
It seems fair to ask why elevators
Are undeservedly given the shaft.

In England the problem is similar,
Although there they call it a lift.
Again, half of its work is unrecognized,
So each car feels predictably miffed.

Here is your chance to gain fortune and fame:
Give this useful device a more fitting name,
One with two directions rather than just one —
A simple-sounding task, but easier said than done.

Pete

Pete chose a name for his bird dog
That sounds odd but decidedly fits.
The dog refused to retrieve, so
Pete said "I'm calling it Quits."

Faith

Faith's college track team was good;
They were champs, to use the vernacular.
When she won the high jump, a fan said
"That leap of Faith was spectacular."

Variety

Readers of poems are often surprised
When words counter their anticipation,
But that's why the rhyme is different each time,
Which we call diversification.

Waving Hello

They met on the boat one fall morning,
Gliding across the river to the city.
She thought "It's like riding a bus on the water."
He thought, "She's remarkably pretty."

A friend said "Their union was ordained,
They were soul mates, certain to endure.
They bonded on that trip twice a day –
It was a ferry tale romance, to be sure."

The Skill Set

Betty's lover was impressed with her talents,
And dismayed when she found someone new.
When he asked why she couldn't be faithful,
She said "I'm just too good to be true."

The Painter's Eye

In the middle ages an artist came upon
A peasant resting on a greensward.
He thought, this scene would make a nice painting,
I could call it "Serf and Turf."

Snookered

Others were stunned when I beat them at 9-ball,
Never suspecting my hidden erudition.
They missed my copy of "How to Win at Pool"
As I carried only the pocket edition.

Clever Hands

A local potter named Kathy was famous for
Glazes that were known far and wide.
Though she modestly avoided self-promotion,
Her creations filled the city with pride.

Always hard at work in her studio,
Making beautiful vases day by day,
Surprised when one earned a first prize,
Cited as an outstanding feat of clay.

Here's To You

I once learned from a phrase book
Although I don't like to boast
That the phrase "a votre sante"
Is one way to say "French toast."

Protection

Vince was a bookie's enforcer
Whose actions were quite reprehensible,
But a bodyguard hired by his victims
Managed to make them invincible.

Into The Sunset

When the horse thief was caught by a posse,
He explained that he had an excuse.
So they promised they wouldn't hang him,
And he said "Thanks. No noose is good noose."

I'll Have Seconds, Please

To observe the passage of time,
It's easiest to study a clock.
Unsurprisingly, that's how I learned
The past tense of <u>tick</u> is, of course, <u>tock</u>.

A friend gave Sharon a new clock,
And she enjoyed hearing it chime.
She said "I'm glad it came as a gift,
Since there's no present like the time."

Grace

Grace had admirable virtues, but she
Dropped things all over the place.
When items were found on the floor,
You can bet they had fallen from Grace.

Tom

Last night Tom drank too much wine.
This morning he said "Close the drapes –
The light makes my hangover worse,
And I suffer from the wrath of grapes."

Valentines

Other Men's Dreams

Some men yearn to take the sun
in retirement on Tahiti.
Others long to be the one
to eliminate graffiti.

Some may want a new cell phone
with features comprehensible.
Others wish they could be known
as manly and invincible.

Some may hope they'll get to drive
a racy Lamborghini,
or have a chance to scuba-dive
with models in bikinis.

But I don't need these nice distractions.
I have other satisfactions.
I don't need a trip or a car;
You're my fantasy, the way you are.

To The Woman Of The Year

Winter, summer, spring and fall –
In every season, you're my all.
Summer, winter, fall and spring,
It's true you are my everything.

When days are warm or when they're raw,
You pull the splinter from my paw.
In pleasant summer or in winter
I count on you to draw that splinter.

When winds are chilly or it's balmy,
In stressful times you always calm me.
When buds appear or leaves add color
You're the icing on my cruller.

In every month you are my favorite.
My life tastes rich because you flavor it.
So stick around – you know I'd miss you.
If you'll stand close I'd like to kiss you.

To My Misnamed Love

Your parents named you, as your kin,
and that was fine with me, but then
I thought of all the times that you
lift me when I'm tired or blue,
smile or laugh when times are tough,
stop me when I've had enough,
indulge my humor day or night,
forgive an unintended slight;
So all in all it seemed a pity
not to use a name more fitting.
The one that comes to mind is Mary,
because it rhymes with necessary.

Sure Comedy's Hard, But So Is Accounting

How do I love thee? Let me count a way or two.
Well, three. Or more. No, this won't do.
A week's gone by and I'm not through.

The number's getting much too high
To calculate, so I just sigh
And try again to recall why

I started this. And you know what?
The reason doesn't matter but
The counting does. I cannot cut

The list to ten, or even twenty.
The point is that the number's plenty.

Of course I could reduce the list
By leaving off some times we kissed
Causing scenery to be missed,

But I'd rather look for other ways
To cut the list of things to praise.
It may take a thousand days.

It may take years but I don't mind.
The fact is that my love is blind,
Which makes it very hard to find

Things I'll do without. You see,
What really counts is you plus me.

The Pairs Competition

I've just two arms to hold you with,
and to embrace your kin and kith.
I've just two eyes to drink you in
but that's enough to make me grin.

I've just two lips to kiss your face,
or hands, or neck, or anyplace.
I've just two legs to walk with you.
(They creak a bit, but they're not new.)

These pairs all work but seem too few.
I wish for more to dazzle you.
Yet even two can be too many.
Pairs may not be worth a penny.

One may be best when all is done.
One's infinitely more than none.
I've just one heart, but it's not lonely
because it's yours, my one and only.

One Risky Valentine

I dreamed you were walking
and a limo stopped near you.
The driver was talking,
and confided, "*My dear, you
by chance attracted the eye of my boss,
who now desires you at whatever cost.
In fact, he wants you as a wife.
He has thirty now, and endless strife.
He thinks your gentility
might bring him tranquility.
He'd dispose of all the others,
Allotting them among his brothers.*
"*It's true you'd move quite far away,
and have to live there, come what may.
But don't dismiss this out of hand –
consider that it could be grand.
I'll forgive your having doubt
if you'll only hear me out.*

"You'd have lots of peace and quiet,
and you'd never have to diet.
You'd have diamonds from Tiffany's,
surprising epiphanies,
soothing baths replete with bubbles,
therapists to ease your troubles,
gorgeous rooms in several palaces,
tea parties as profound as Alice's,
private jets to ease your travel,
cashmeres that would never ravel,
heated pools to aid your swimming,
skirts that never needed hemming,
servants at your beck and call,
masterpieces on your wall,
closets of designer gowns,
jesters to erase your frowns.
To me that sounds like quite a lot.
I hope that you'll give it some thought."

And in my dream, you replied:

"*Of course the offer gives me pause.
I'm of two minds on this because
my husband can't provide all that
but knows I hate to wear a hat.
He knows I read myself to sleep.
He knows what souvenirs I keep.
He likes the way I style my hair.
He's glad to take me everywhere.
One thing that's fairly rare to see:
His pleasure comes from pleasing me.
He's not so bad as husbands go,
so my answer must be no.*"

My dream thus ended with relief,
and I was spared impending grief.
I knew you wouldn't start to pack
when you walked in and said "I'm back."

Valentine's Day, Back So Soon

I can't believe another year has passed.
The wing'd chariot now has the speed of light,
Made faster because we are together
Morning, noon and (blessedly) at night.

So long ago it seems the die was cast
That made us one, and proved so right.
Bonded so we have no need of tether –
Even miles apart, somehow still in sight.

The odds now say we two will last,
Seeing each other as Lady and Knight.
That will be true regardless of whether
It gets even better, as I think it might.

I know it sounds strange, this fancy, my flight:
In my mind's eye your gown will always be white.

Who Knew?

The first time that we met
those many years ago
I said to myself
she's pretty, and smart, and funny, and sexy
(maybe not in that order)
but it took me far too long
to see the light

I didn't know then
that your lips or your heart
would be so soft
or that they would stay that way
for life

I didn't know then
that seeing things through your eyes
would open mine

I didn't know then
how good it would feel
to tell friends or strangers
"This is my wife"

I didn't know then
that all these years later
I would still be impressed
and still in love

Yes, I Take It Personally

This started as a kind of ode,
intended as a hymn of praise
with fulsome words of gratitude
for a multitude of days

That passed too quickly, racing by
instead of pausing to be savored
by the aging lovesick swain
whom you and fate unduly favored.

Instead, the verse took quite a turn
when this thought came to me:
I'm glad not just for what you are
but what you've helped me be.

I've felt things I wouldn't have felt
and seen things I wouldn't have seen.
I've learned things I wouldn't have learned
and discovered what loving can mean.

Of course, you know I'm grateful that
you are the way you are —
huggable and kissable,
and still my shining star.

But because you make me better
in more ways than I can measure,
I add these names to you alone:
my love, my sweet, my treasure.

Hearthrob

Do you get to my aorta? Well, sorta.
Do you really think I'd letcha? You betcha.

Wondering, Wondering

Artists take pride in their skill
But sometimes feel diminished
If they're unable to decide
Just when their work is finished.

> "I think this portrait's done.
> Does it need a few more touches?
> What will I say if critics ask
> Is that the Duke, or Duchess?"

> "My play has crucial dialogue
> In need of more revisions.
> Or maybe not. Odds bodkins,
> How I hate these late decisions."

> "My symphony is much too long.
> I know it should be shorter.
> But should I cut it by a third
> Or only by a quarter?"

Yes, creators earn our sympathy
When lost in introspection,
Wondering when they should stop
Because they've reached perfection.

But once an artist chose just right
And knew that she had won.
She took a look when you were born
And smiled, and said "I'm done."

Let's Move Valentine's Day

Here's a Valentine verse, for once,
That doesn't mention hearts. The months
Of May and June are made for loving,
But February calls for moving
Toward a love more kind and gentle,
Rather less physical than mental,
Of tender touches and holding hands,
Of violins rather than brass bands,
Of huddling underneath the covers
More for warmth than being lovers.
If that should someday be our fate,
Believe me, sweetheart, I can wait.
February is still a bummer.
I long expectantly for summer.

Let's Look Back

Three billion women on the earth,
But one was meant for me.
Fortune smiled when you appeared
And changed my "I" to "we."

Many years have passed since then,
Which some might find appalling.
Yet things that happened in those years
Are clearly worth recalling.

Satchel Paige said don't look back
'cause something might be gaining.
I side with Proust, and hope you find
Our memories entertaining.

Prothalamion For Us

A shared glance, a quick understanding
Knowing each other's thoughts
Before they become words

Watch them together and you know
They hug and kiss every morning
And smile at the same things
Until time to kiss goodnight

They remember times of joy
And times of sorrow
And small children growing up
Entirely too fast

Years of touching
Even when apart
This is clearly a love story
With chapters to come

Tom Swifties

Tom Swift was the young hero of a series of books published between 1910 and 1935. As written, the character seldom just "said" anything, but did so with a modifier: "madly," "softly," "eagerly," and so on. This excess led to parody versions of such statements, naturally called Tom Swifties. Here are my additions to the world's growing collection.

I made this boat myself, said Tom craftily.
I do a pretty good Stallone impression, said Tom slyly.
This area never has earthquakes, said Tom faultlessly.
This carton holds 144 of the items, said Tom grossly.
I'm tired of long prayers before meals, said Tom gracefully.
My kids are afraid of the Santa at the mall, said Tom claustrophobically.
Her eyebrows look kind of odd, Tom said archly.
Our house has paintings on every wall, said Tom artfully.
The hay in the barn is stacked to the ceiling, said Tom balefully.
I've never been a fan of fairy tales, Tom noted grimly.

This seance seems to be working, said Tom raptly.
Sorry I can't pay you what I owe, said Tom shyly.
Exams don't really measure student progress, Tom said testily.
I have no idea how deep the river is, said Tom unfathomably.
That sounds like a kazoo, said Tom astutely.
The lye soap is eating the laundry, said Tom caustically.
We keep the dangerous animals in here, Tom said cagily.
What a lovely tune, exclaimed Tom airily.
The Apaches are welcome here, said Tom bravely.
My tailor is truly talented, exclaimed Tom fitfully.

This outfit was worn by Sister Martha, enunciated Tom habitually.
This lot holds a hundred rental cars, said Tom fleetingly.
I got the gun away from him, said Tom disarmingly.
I counterfeited a passable five-dollar bill, said Tom ably.
I have to do this first, said Dr. Swift harmlessly.
This apartment feels quite spacious, said Tom loftily.
The concept of infinity fascinates me, Tom repeated endlessly.
I can't stand New England poets, said Tom frostily.
I admire Ayn Rand's work, Tom stated objectively.
I'm a Teamster and proud of it, stated Tom truculently.

We have poison ivy in the yard, Tom observed rashly.
Looks like your drive missed the fairway, Tom chided roughly.
I certainly miss San Francisco, said Tom heartlessly.
This singing group has overstayed its welcome, Tom said gleefully.
We're moving the prisoners downstairs, said Tom condescendingly.
Nobody beats the casino all the time, said Tom winsomely.
I've forgotten the lyrics, but I remember the tune, said Tom humbly.
Remind me, who was Fred's partner?, Tom asked gingerly.
I must have walked every street in Paris, Tom said ruefully.
My family is fated to do great things, said Tom clandestinely.

Part of a loaf is better than none, said Tom affably.
Writing assignments give me a pain, Tom said prosaically.
The bee shortage means fewer flowers this spring, Tom said lackadaisically.
I'm sorry the legal work cost so much, Tom apologized feebly.

Putting baking soda in the fridge killed the odor, Tom said distinctly.
Let's get married, Tom said engagingly.
Next we'll get divorced, Tom said despairingly.
I do public relations work for Exxon, Tom said crudely.
I feel you're a good friend, Tom said palpably.
I'm converting prose to poetry, Tom said inversely.

We helped save two lions in Africa, Tom said pridefully.
I can hit the target with my eyes closed, Tom asserted aimlessly.
I dislike using letters in place of four-letter words, Tom said ineffably.
I'm not sure what kind of article that is, Tom said indefinitely.
What an adorable baby, Tom said awesomely and acutely.
Boy, that is one sour apple, said Tom tartly.
These look like stolen goods to me, Tom said mistakenly.
Camping out is kind of fun, Tom said intently.
I'm a victim of identity theft, said Tom selflessly.
I've opened the peaches and pears, said Tom uncannily.
I've started learning the Greek letters, Tom said alphabetically.

I'm presently committed to using decimals, Tom said tensely.

We're confining the felons in their order of arrest, Tom said consequently.

Is this one of the Great Lakes?, asked Tom eerily.

My pants are falling apart, said Tom seamlessly.

The USO shows just aren't the same without Bob, said Tom hopelessly.

Thanks anyway, I've got plenty, Tom said needlessly.

Can somebody give me a light?, Tom asked matchlessly.

I know where to steal a stole, said Tom furtively.

I deserve every dollar I make, said Tom earnestly.

My estate planning is done, said Tom willingly.

The buzzers and chimes get on my nerves, said Tom alarmingly.

It's my turn to be on sentry duty, said Tom haltingly.

My head is just bursting with ideas, said Tom mindfully.

I'm letting people in to see the national tennis match, Tom admitted openly.

The toast is way overdone, Tom complained crisply.

My red suspenders are both showy and effective, Tom said bracingly.

My friends are always borrowing money, said Tom touchingly.
Charlie Chan will never solve this one, said Tom cluelessly.
I can't stop thinking about Batman and Dracula, said Tom inescapably.

Oops – I'm going to be tagged out, said Tom baselessly.
There are too many cows in this pasture, Tom complained movingly.
We haven't cleaned out the fireplace all winter, Tom said gratefully.
I like the subjects of sentences best, Tom announced.
I can make you an amulet in my workshop, said Tom charmingly.
I'm on in five minutes, where are my notes? Tom asked speechlessly.
There's an example of good dental work, Tom said evenly.
What's wrong with smoking pot? asked Tom stonily.
I prefer the term "eccentric," Tom said oddly.
Looks like you may get some cavities soon, said Tom precariously.

Now that I'm elected, let's pass some laws, said Tom incongruously.

I'm something of a demolition expert, said Tom profusely.

Waiter, how about a compliment instead of a tip?, Tom asked gratuitously.

I'm going to cook some hamburgers, Tom said flippantly.

I've had it up to here with loud parties, said Tom bashfully.

I tend to be Aristotelian, Tom said moderately.

Sorry I couldn't get here on time, said Tom belatedly.

Your room is a real mess, said Tom stylishly.

We seem to have sailed into the Sargasso Sea, Tom said calmly.

I'm looking for the men's room, Tom said gently.

My pencil broke again, Tom said pointlessly.

I just got out of the shower, said Tom starkly.

I'd be glad to travel with you, said Tom companionably.

In-vitro fertilization didn't work in this case, said Tom inconceivably.

Electronic control boards are too complex for me, said Tom inconsolably.

This is too heavy for me to carry, said Tom unbearably.

Let's watch "Leave It to Beaver," said Tom eagerly.

This parking meter accepts phony quarters, said Tom sluggishly.
Have a seat, offered Tom charitably.
I'm hurrying to the bathroom, said Tom peevishly.

I enjoy "Saturday Night Live," said Tom skittishly.
Are these tombs found everywhere under Rome?, Tom asked cryptically.
Our senator seems to have been in office forever, said Tom interminably.
I play my guitar from dawn to dusk, said Tom fretfully.
I've learned only one of the new dances, said Tom frugally.
We're not ready to go to the supermarket yet, said Tom listlessly.
What's so bad about an erratic heartbeat?, asked Tom impulsively.
Please, no more apples or bananas, Tom pleaded fruitfully.
SOS! SOS! Tom radioed helplessly.
Boy, that is one sour apple, said Tom tartly.

I prefer unposed pictures of people, said Tom candidly.
We've all got to stick together, said Tom coherently.
Let's put that off until later, said Tom deferentially.

We don't run ads here at NPR, said Tom spotlessly.
The storm must have knocked out the phones,
Tom said tonelessly.
I'm not sure what kind of article that is, said Tom
indefinitely.
Fuel from bogs can be used over and over again,
Tom said repeatedly.
Yum, four-and-twenty blackbirds baked into a pie,
said Tom ravenously.
I lost all my money in the crash, said Tom
unfortunately.
This could be from the Ming dynasty, or maybe
not, said Tom evasively.

These erotic drawings are almost pathological,
Tom said illustriously.
I buy gas here every week, Tom said regularly.
We'll take one of these, and two of these, Tom said
selectively.
It just looks like a mouse to me, Tom said
shrewdly.
Fido runs to the door every time the bell rings,
said Tom dogmatically.
The cops took my neighbor in, Tom said
arrestingly.
The Red Sox will never beat the Yankees now, Tom
said ruthlessly.
People talk funny in these Brooklyn bars, Tom said
disjointedly.
Okay, I take it all back, said Tom unspeakably.

I played four sports in college, Tom said jocularly.
Tonight's performance has been canceled, Tom announced disconcertingly.
Don't sway from side to side when you walk, Tom pleaded hypnotically.
I hope your good fortune will come back, Tom said reluctantly.
I'm afraid we don't have many, Tom said futilely.
This trail is the only way to get back, Tom said pathologically.
I wrote a poem for a commercial, Tom said adversely.
The utility got our power back on, Tom said revoltingly.
That's a nice painting of a trout, said Tom artificially.
We'll need more candles for your birthday cake, Tom said wickedly.

I may never see how these mini-programs work, Tom said apprehensively.
I'm in favor of action words, Tom said proverbially.
I may be getting a tetanus shot, Tom said hypothetically.
That is one unattractive girl, Tom said dismissively.
They electrocuted two criminals at the same time, Tom said concurrently.

The mechanic said my tailpipe was clogged, Tom said inexhaustibly.
It wasn't cheap, but we got him out of prison, said Tom expensively.
These shore birds fly a lot like eagles, Tom said gullibly.
No, officer, I won't take the test, Tom said breathlessly.
It still looks like lab glassware to me, Tom retorted.

You'll go to the rear of the ship and stay there, Tom said sternly.
The election had to be cancelled, Tom reported devotedly.
My golf drives were all great today, Tom bragged tediously.
I'm going to bed early tonight, said Tom attentively.
I'm not going to pay that bill, Tom said unremittingly.
Of course there's only one way to close a prayer, said Tom amenably.
For once that lawyer's argument was short, Tom reported briefly.
Speeding tickets here are expensive, Tom complained finally.
I was the first one to ask her to the school dance, Tom said promptly.

The doctor says I'll be here for three more days, Tom said patiently.

Our police department staff is finally complete, said Tom forcefully.
The referee is counting him out, Tom said intentionally.
Blackjack! yelled Tom tenaciously.
I think I'm finally catching on, Tom said graspingly.

About the Author

Dr. James W. Swinehart is a social psychologist who has worked for the U.S. Army (Counter Intelligence Corps, Korea); Washington University (sociology department); University of Michigan (Survey Research Center, School of Public Health, Highway Safety Research Institute); Children's Television Workshop; TV networks (CBS, NBC, PBS); numerous federal agencies (e.g., Social Security Administration, National Cancer Institute, Federal Trade Commission, Library of Congress); national nonprofit organizations (e.g., American Medical Association, National Safety Council, Association for Consumer Research); and other similar groups. He has served on the boards of several public interest organizations.

In addition to teaching social science at universities, he has taught swimming and water safety for the Red Cross and a college, and English as a second language overseas. He has traveled in 47 states and 20 countries, sometimes by moped or hitchhiking. A photographer, his greatest pride is his two sons and four grandchildren.

About the Publisher

The Sager Group was founded in 1984. In 2012 it was chartered as a multimedia content brand, with the intent of empowering those who create art—an umbrella beneath which makers can pursue, and profit from, their craft directly, without gatekeepers. TSG publishes books; ministers to artists and provides modest grants; and produces documentary, feature, and commercial films. By harnessing the means of production, The Sager Group helps artists help themselves. For more information, please see TheSagerGroup.net.

More Books from The Sager Group

Mandela was Late: Odd Things & Essays From the Seinfeld Writer Who Coined Yada, Yada and Made Spongeworthy a Compliment
by Peter Mehlman

#MeAsWell, A Novel
by Peter Mehlman

The Orphan's Daughter, A Novel
by Jan Cherubin

*Words to Repair the World:
Stories of Life, Humor and Everyday Miracles*
by Mike Levine

Miss Havilland, A Novel by Gay Daly

*Revenge of the Donut Boys:
True Stories of Lust, Fame, Survival and Multiple Personality*
By Mike Sager

Lifeboat No. 8: Surviving the Titanic
by Elizabeth Kaye

See our entire library at TheSagerGroup.net

www.ingramcontent.com/pod-product-compliance
Lightning Source LLC
Chambersburg PA
CBHW030321100526
44592CB00010B/512